Rosemary Davids a

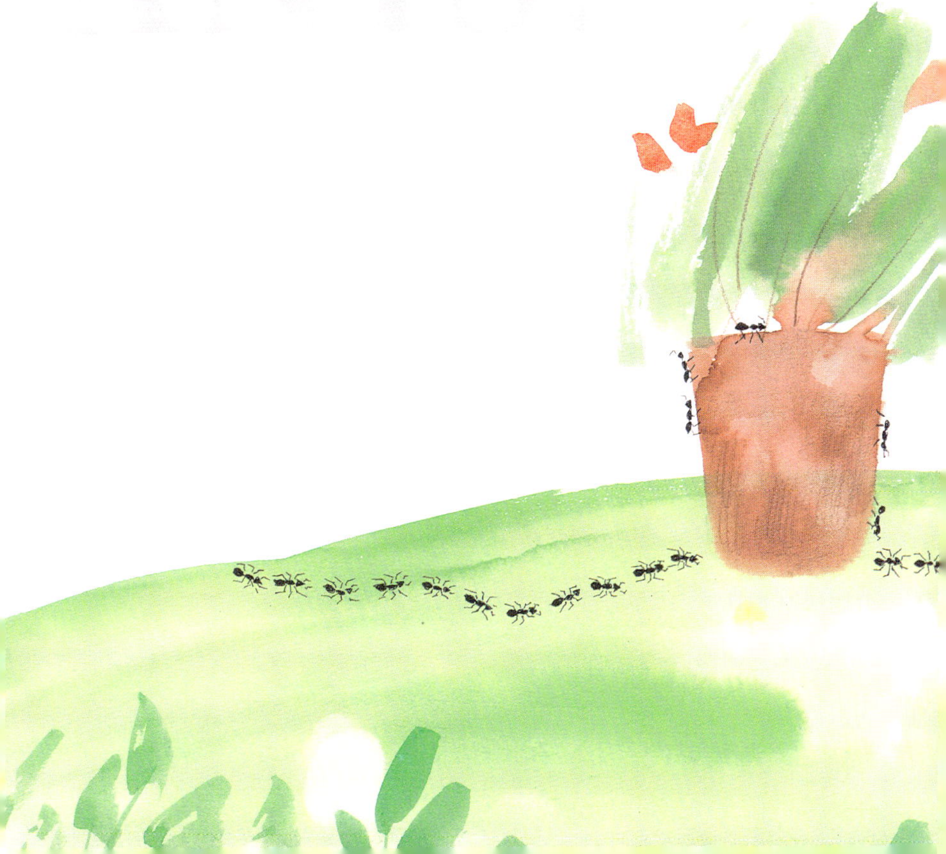

Ants in the garden.

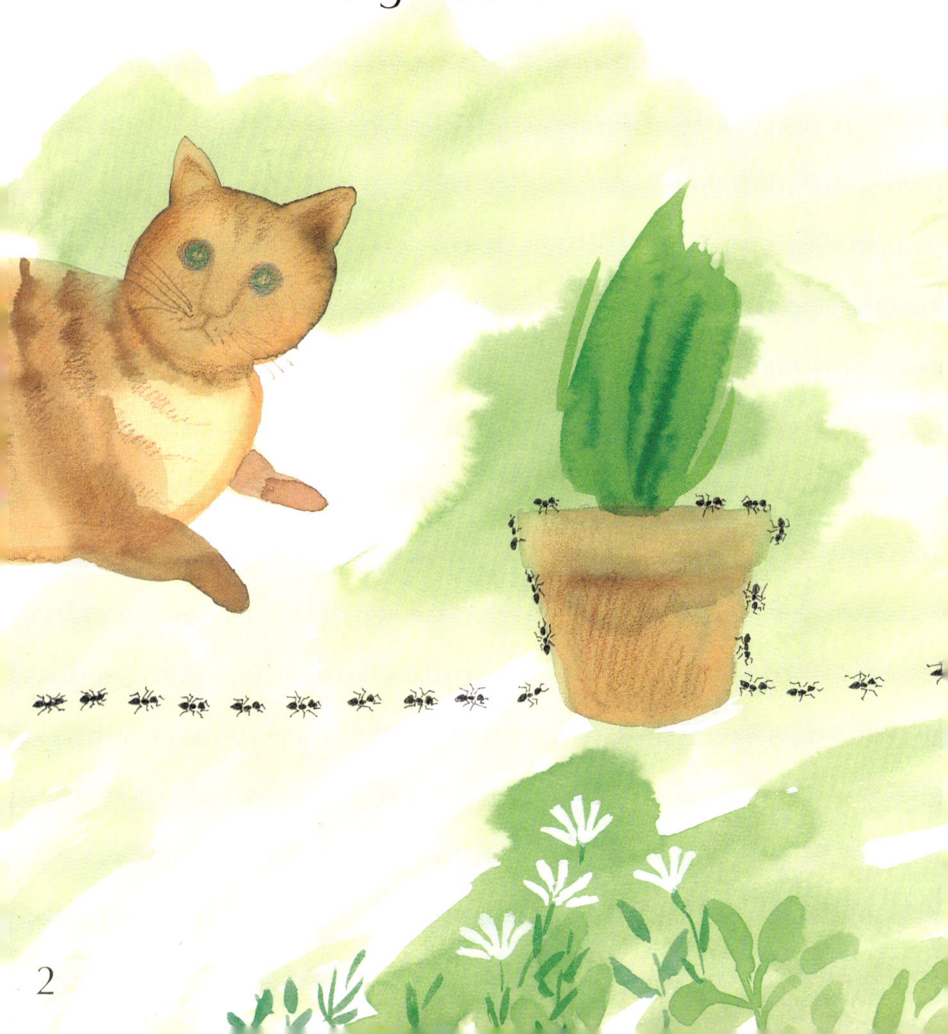

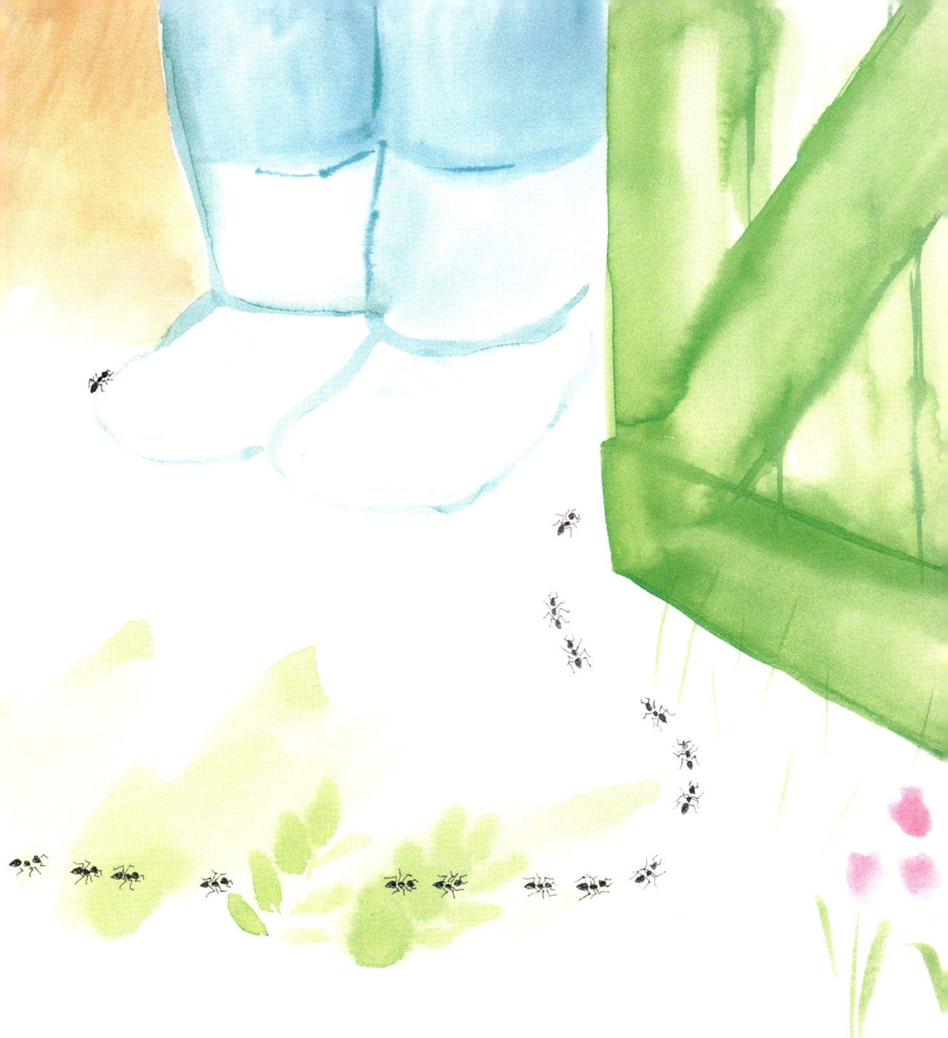

Ants in the shed.

Ants
in the
kitchen.

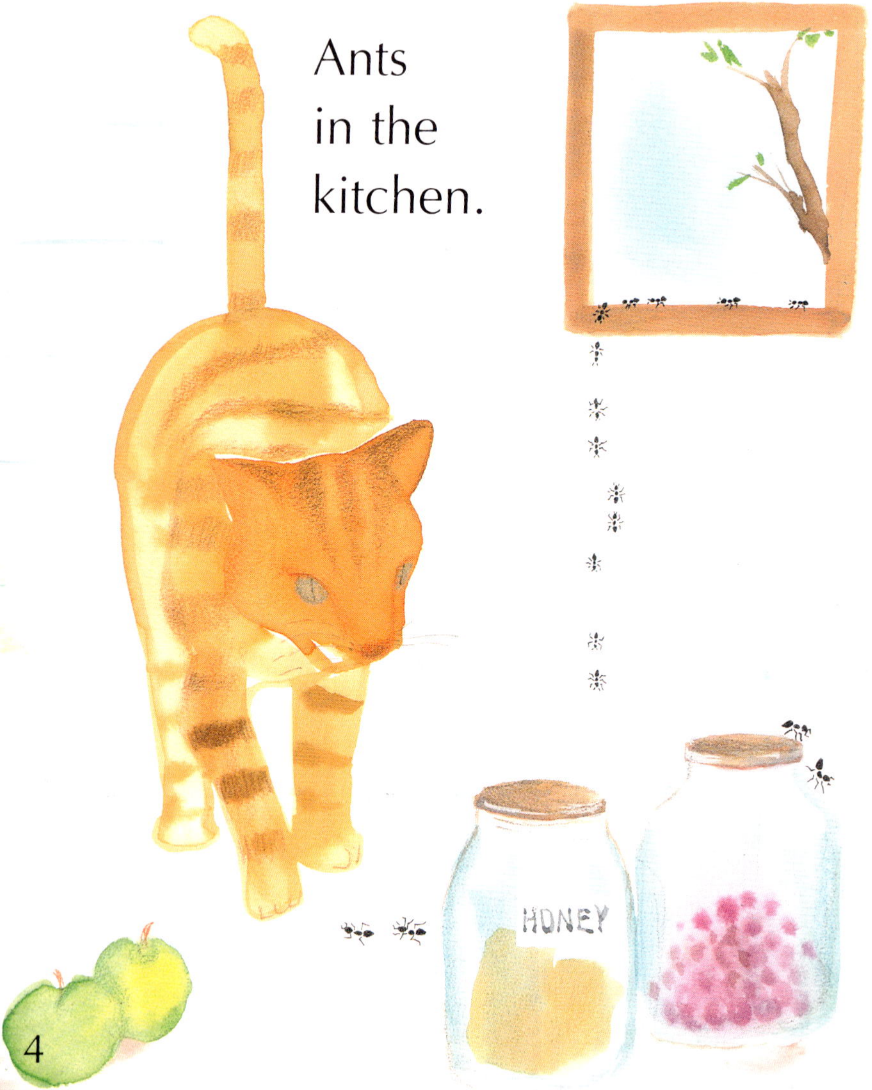

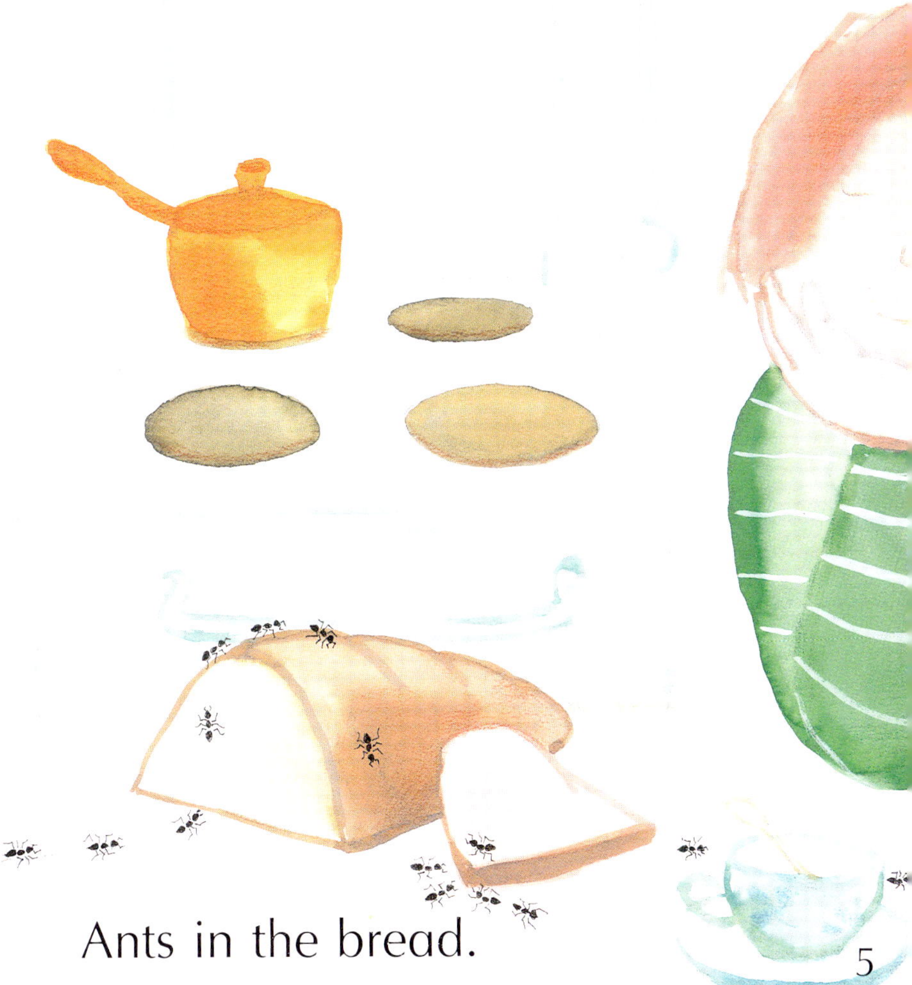

Ants in the bread.

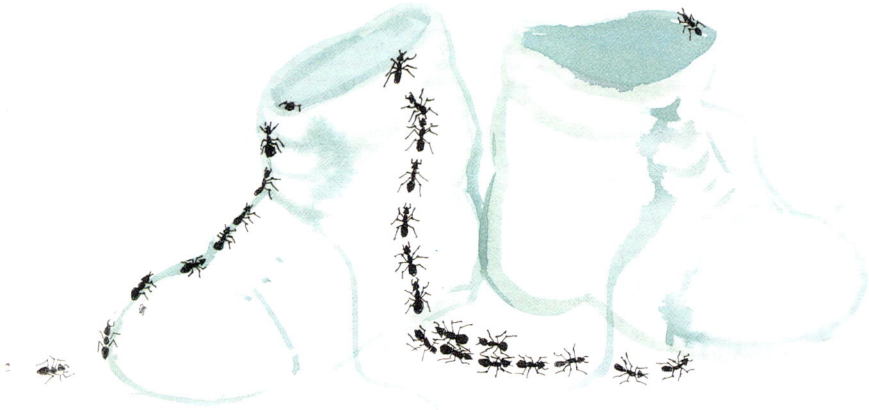

Ants busy crawling.
Ants that are dead.

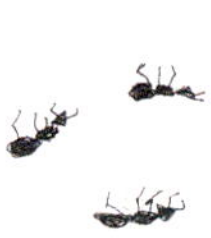

Ants in the bedroom.

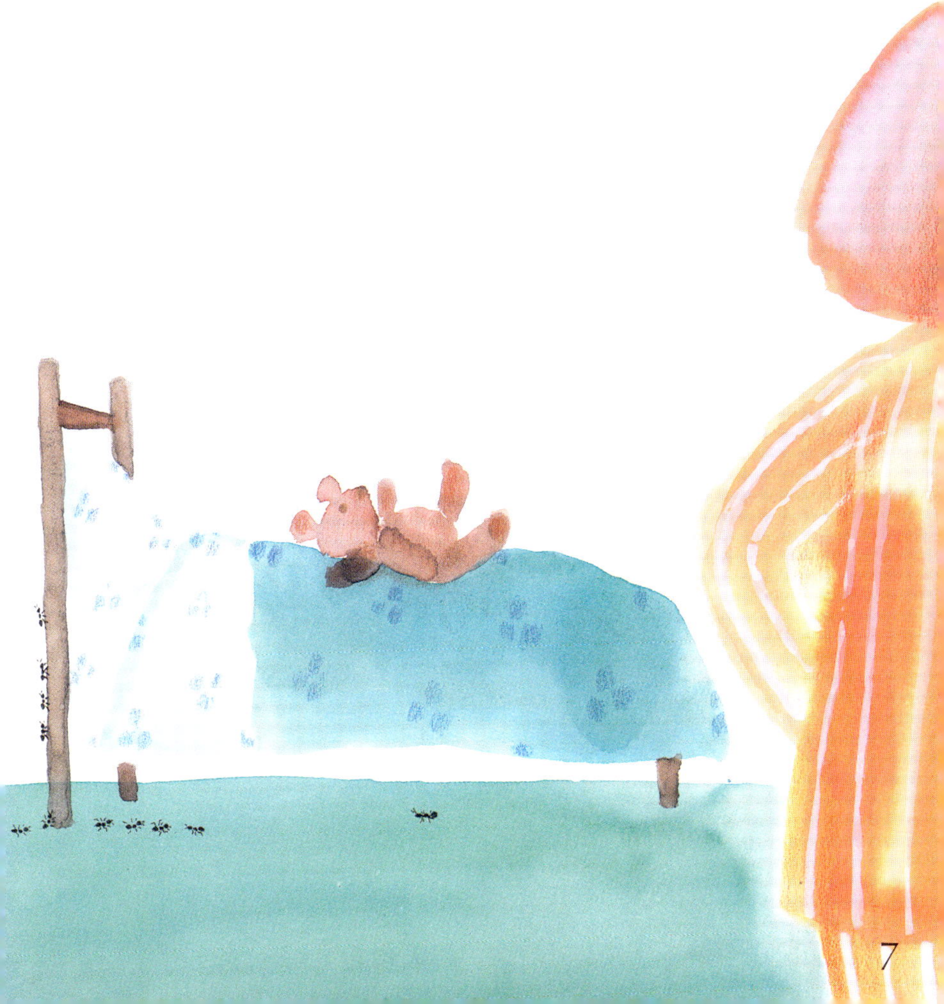

Ants in the bed!

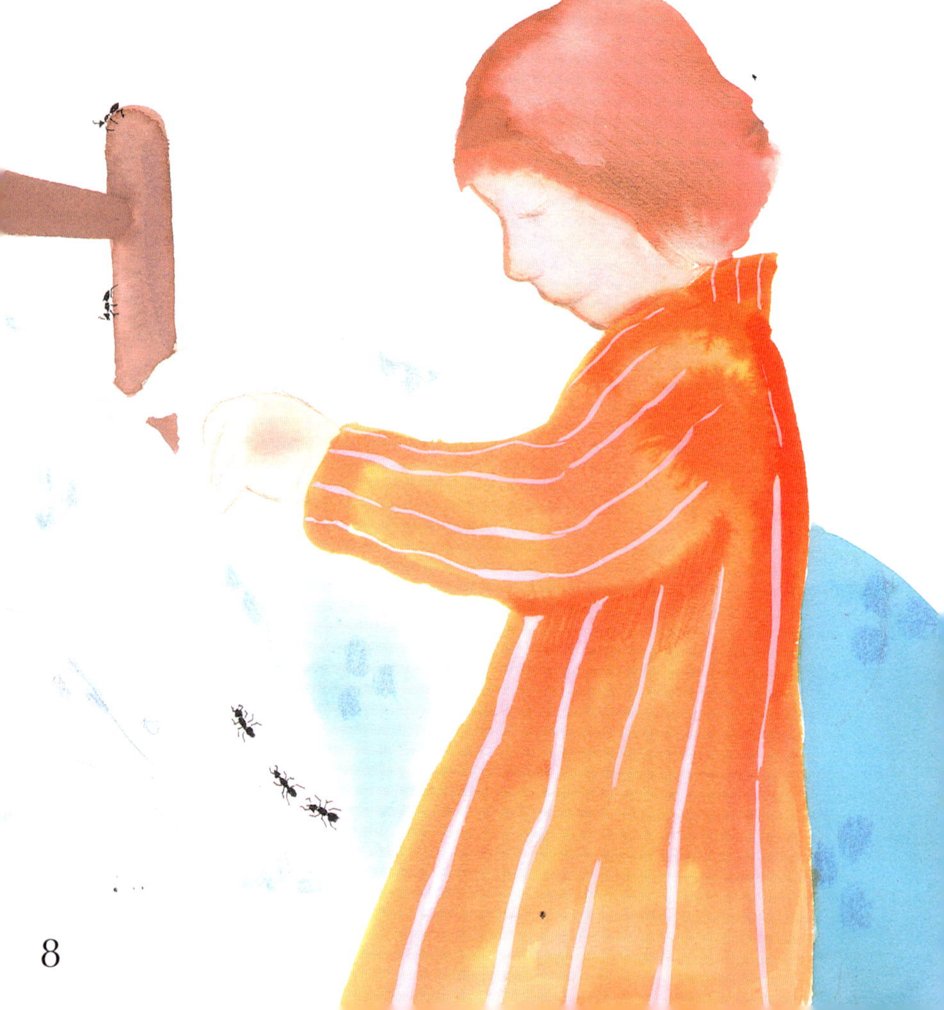